WEATHER AND CLIMATE

WIDE WORLD OF WEATHER

WEATHER AND CLIMATE AROUND THE WORLD

Emily Raij

Raintree is an imprint of Capstone Global Library Limited, a company incorporated in England and Wales having its registered office at 264 Banbury Road, Oxford, OX2 7DY – Registered company number: 6695582

www.raintree.co.uk
myorders@raintree.co.uk

Edited by Erika L. Shores
Designed by Tracey McCabe
Original illustrations © Capstone Global Library Limited 2021
Media research by Kelly Garvin
Premedia by Kathy McColley
Originated by Capstone Global Library Ltd
Printed and bound in India

978 1 4747 9355 1 (hardback)
978 1 4747 9731 3 (paperback)

British Library Cataloguing in Publication Data
A full catalogue record for this book is available from the British Library.

Acknowledgements
We would like to thank the following for permission to reproduce photographs: Shutterstock: iStockphoto/zhongguo, cover (bottom left); Shutterstock: Adwo, 8, Alessandro Zappalorto, 21, Alex Lerner, 19, Cre8 design, cover (top left), fokke baarssen, 29, FootageLab, 20, Gerhard Strydom, cover (bottom right), guentermanaus, 10, I. Noyan Yilmaz, 25, Jarmo Piironen, 15, jejiim, 13, John D Sirlin, cover (bottom right), Jon Ingall, 12, juerginho, 27, Kodda, 26, Konstantnin, 18, Maciej Czekajewski, 11, Mo Wu, 4, Nym3ria, 5, Oleksandr Katrusha, 23, Rawpixel.com, 28, risteski goce, 22, Sander van der Werf, cover (top right), 1, Soleil Nordic, 7, Tarpan, 9, 16, Troutnut, 17, vladsilver, 24. Artistic elements: Shutterstock; gigi rosa, MaddyZ, Rebellion Works.

CONTENTS

Words in **bold** are in the glossary.

CHAPTER 1

WEATHER AND CLIMATE

Whoosh! Wind is howling outside. Snow is falling heavily. It's a cold winter's night in London. No one wants to go outside. Across the world in the country of Australia, it's a different story. The sun is shining. Temperatures are rising. Beaches are full of people. How can the weather be so different on the same planet and at the same time?

People gather on sandy beaches during summer on Australia's coasts.

Weather is what's happening in the **atmosphere** from day to day. Wind and temperature are weather conditions that can change all the time.

Climate is the average weather conditions over a very long period of time. There are many factors affecting climate. The way these factors affect climate is different in each region, or part, of the world. That's why each region has its own climate.

Snow piles up during a blizzard in New York City.

Many things affect the climate of a place. How close an area is to a large body of water is one factor. Ocean and wind **currents**, or movements, also affect climate. The features of the land and the height of land above sea level are two more factors.

One of the biggest effects on a location's climate is its **latitude**. That is an area's distance from the **equator**. The equator is a made-up line that divides Earth into northern and southern halves.

Earth's **axis** is always tilting the same way. This causes the Sun to shine more or less on different areas at different times. Our different seasons occur as Earth moves around the Sun.

Because Earth's axis is tilted, locations closer to the equator get more direct sunlight throughout the year. These places are called the tropics. They have warmer climates than places further from the equator.

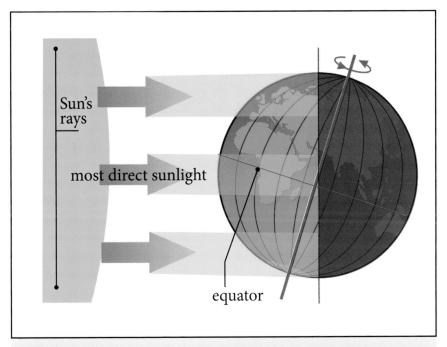

During the day, areas along the equator receive more direct sunlight. This is because the areas are closer to the Sun than the northern and southern parts of Earth.

CHAPTER 2

DIFFERENT CLIMATE TYPES

A climate is based on temperature, how much and when **precipitation** happens and what grows in the area. The main climate types are desert, tropical, temperate and polar.

DESERT CLIMATE

Desert climates are dry. They get fewer than 25 centimetres of precipitation a year. The air in a desert holds less moisture than in wetter climates. Desert air has less water. There is not enough water to contain the day's heat. That means nights are cold. The big change in temperature from day to night makes it hard to live in desert climates.

FACT

The driest spot outside Antarctica is the Atacama Desert in northern Chile. A city in this desert went without water for 400 years!

Many deserts get very hot. Some deserts can reach 50 degrees Celsius. But not all deserts are hot. Antarctica is a desert. It is the coldest place on Earth. But it doesn't rain or snow very much. Antarctica has the coldest, windiest and driest climate in the world.

The icy Antarctic desert

TROPICAL CLIMATE

Tropical climates are hot all year. Their average temperature is above 18° Celsius.

Rainforests are tropical climates with lots of rain. They get between 127 and 635 cm of rain every year. One example is the Amazon rainforest in South America. It is the world's biggest rainforest. More than half of the world's types of plants and animals live in rainforests. Plants grow well in the warm, wet air.

The Amazon rainforest is in Brazil. Brazil is in South America.

Other tropical climates are hot all year but have a wet and dry season. These areas are called **savannahs**. Africa has many savannahs. Tall grasses grow in savannahs. Plants and trees can survive in **droughts** there. North and South America and Australia also have savannahs.

A savannah in the African country of Kenya

TEMPERATE CLIMATE

Temperate climates are usually not too hot and not too cold. The average temperature in a temperate climate is warmer than 10° Celsius. There is also not a lot of rain or snow through the year. Temperate climates get an average of 30 cm to 200 cm of rain a year. But daily temperatures and weather can change quite a lot. One day it might be hot and sunny. The next day there could be rain and it might feel cold.

Plants grow well near the Mediterranean Sea.

There are different types of temperate climates. One type of temperate climate is affected by sea winds and currents. Areas near the Mediterranean Sea have warm, dry summers and short, rainy winters. It doesn't get very cold. Western Europe and western North America have this type of climate, too. Mild temperatures mean lots of plants can grow here.

California's coast is along the Pacific Ocean. It has a temperate climate.

Continental is a type of temperate climate. Places with continental climates have four seasons. Spring is warm and wet. Summer is hot and fairly dry. Autumn is cool and dry. Winters are cold with snow and lots of wind.

The midwestern United States, southern Canada and central Europe have continental climates. It can rain or snow all year round. There is enough moisture for many trees and plants to grow. Most trees in continental climates lose their leaves in autumn and winter.

Another type of temperate climate is **subarctic**. It has long, very cold winters and short, cool summers. Much of Alaska, Canada, Russia and Iceland is subarctic. Most of these areas have little precipitation.

A HUGE FOREST

The boreal forest has a subarctic climate. It spreads across many countries. These include Canada, Alaska in the United States, Russia, Norway, Sweden, Finland and even parts of Japan. It makes up one-third of the world's forest area.

The trees of the boreal forest cover much of Finland in northern Europe.

POLAR CLIMATE

The polar climate at the North and South Poles is freezing! The North Pole, or Arctic, is surrounded by the Arctic Ocean with floating sheets of ice. The South Pole is on Antarctica. The land here is covered in thick ice. The average winter temperature in the Arctic is -34° Celsius. At the South Pole, it's -60° Celsius.

Although snow is rare, it builds up over long periods of time in Antarctica.

The sun shines all day from March through to September at the North Pole, and all day from September through to March at the South Pole. Most of the Arctic is too cold and dry for trees to grow. But during summer, a thin layer of soil thaws. Grass grows. Yellow poppies bloom, too. At the South Pole, some small plants grow in places that are not always covered in snow and ice.

Only small plants are found in the freezing Arctic.

CHAPTER 3

LIFE IN DIFFERENT CLIMATES

DESERT LIFE

Desert plants and animals can live with little water and extreme heat. The cactus stores water in its stem. Other plants and flowers only bloom when it rains. Desert foxes get the liquid they need from eating other animals. To keep cool during the day, many desert animals stay underground or under rocks. They hunt only during the cooler night.

FACT

Camels do well in deserts. Camels have two rows of eyelashes. They also have nostrils that close. Both keep out sand. Fat stored in their humps lets them go days without food and water.

People have found ways to survive living in hot deserts. The Bedouin tribe of the Middle East lives in tents. The cloth walls allow air to flow. Tents are lined with animal hair. This keeps heat and cold in or out when needed.

Cacti grow in the deserts of the southwestern United States.

TROPICAL LIFE

Trees in tropical rainforests grow tall. Their branches and leaves stretch out to form a **canopy**, or cover, over the forest. When a dead tree falls, it lets in sunlight. Then a new tree can grow. The canopy is also home to many animals. Colourful birds fill the trees. Monkeys swing from high branches.

A tropical rainforest

Some people live in rainforests. They hunt and fish rainforest animals. They eat fruits and nuts from rainforest plants. Some people grow their own food.

Houses in tropical places are sometimes built on stilts. This stops water flooding homes. Stilts also let breezes flow under the houses to cool them.

A house on stilts in the Amazon rainforest

TEMPERATE LIFE

Plants in temperate climates must survive dry summers. Pine, cypress and oak trees are found here. Olive, fig, grape and citrus trees also grow well. There are small shrubs and herbs but not large patches of grass. That means animals, such as goats, sheep and rabbits, can't eat only grass. They must eat other plants, too.

In continental forests, trees change with the seasons. Trees lose their leaves when temperatures get cold in autumn and winter. They grow again in warm spring weather.

Olive trees grow in temperate climates.

Many animals are suited to life in climates with changing seasons. Black bears have thick fur to stay warm during winter. They go into dens and sleep when it gets very cold. They live off their body fat. Squirrels store food and nest in trees during winter.

Red squirrels live in trees during winter in temperate climates.

POLAR LIFE

Animals such as penguins, seals and fish call Antarctica home. Penguins and seals have a thick layer of fat to stay warm. The blood of some fish is special so they can stay alive in icy waters.

At the North Pole, polar bears are at home. They blend in with the snow. This helps polar bears creep up on and catch other animals to eat.

Penguins dive into the water to hunt for fish.

In Antarctica, at any given time, there are about 75 camps where scientists live and work, studying the Antarctic environment. As many as 1,000 scientists are there in the winter months. In summer, 4,000 scientists work there. There are also places that tourists visit in Antarctica.

A small camp made by scientists near the South Pole

CHAPTER 4

HOW IS CLIMATE CHANGING?

Changes in the world's climate are making it harder for plants and animals to survive. People are the biggest cause of this change. Burning **fossil fuels** such as coal, oil and natural gas releases **carbon dioxide** into the air. Fossil fuels are used to power cars and make electricity. Carbon dioxide absorbs heat. Heat gets trapped by Earth's atmosphere and creates warmer temperatures.

A power plant burns coal to make energy.
Burning coal adds carbon dioxide to the air.

Hotter temperatures affect the places where animals live and the food they eat. Sometimes animals move to new areas. But they can't always thrive in their new homes.

Hotter temperatures can cause corn and other crops to die in fields.

A SPREADING DESERT

Rising temperatures are causing dry areas to spread. The Sahara is in Africa. It is the largest warm-weather desert. It has grown in size by 10 per cent since 1920. More heat and less rainfall make it harder to grow food.

Climate change affects every type of climate. Seasons and life cycles have shifted. Precipitation patterns have changed. Some parts of the world get bigger storms. Warmer temperatures mean spring comes earlier in some places. Migrating animals may return before there is food available to eat. In some places there is less water and less good land to grow food. Plants and animals are losing their homes.

Recycling plastic means fewer resources will be used to make new plastic.

LOOKING TO THE FUTURE

Most countries are working to lower how much carbon dioxide they put into the air. Businesses are using more clean energy. This includes energy from the wind and Sun. Using energy made by the wind and the Sun does not add carbon dioxide to the atmosphere. Many people are also trying to reduce their carbon dioxide **pollution**. Some are driving electric cars instead of cars that burn petrol or diesel. They are recycling and reusing everyday items. We can all help protect the climates around the world.

Energy created by wind turbines does not add carbon dioxide to the air.

GLOSSARY

atmosphere mixture of gases that surrounds Earth

axis real or imaginary line through the centre of an object, around which the object turns

canopy middle layer of the rainforest where the greenery is thick and there is little sunlight

carbon dioxide gas that has no smell or colour

climate average weather in a place over many years

current movement of air or of water in a river or an ocean

drought long period of weather with little or no rainfall

equator imaginary line around the middle of Earth; it divides the northern and southern hemispheres

fossil fuel natural fuel formed from the remains of plants and animals over millions of years; coal, oil and natural gas are fossil fuels

latitude distance measured north or south of the equator

pollution substances that make air, land and water dirty and not safe to use

precipitation water that falls from the clouds in the form of rain, hail or snow

savannah flat, grassy area of land with few or no trees

subarctic areas directly south of the Arctic Circle; the Arctic Circle is an imaginary line just south of the North Pole

FIND OUT MORE

BOOKS

Human Environmental Impact: How We Affect Earth (Humans and Our Planet), Ava Sawyer (Raintree, 2018)

Temperate Climates (Focus on Climate Zones), Cath Senker (Raintree, 2018)

Weather Infographics (Infographics), Chris Oxlade (Raintree, 2015)

WEBSITES

www.dkfindout.com/uk/animals-and-nature/habitats-and-ecosystems/
Find out more about different habitats and their climates, including the African savannah, American desert and Amazon rainforest.

www.natgeokids.com/uk/discover/geography/general-geography/what-is-climate-change/
Learn about the causes of climate change, how climate change is affecting Earth and how humans can help to protect the planet.

INDEX